GO AND PLAY
BADMINTON

BAD
Go

GO AND PLAY

BADMINTON

TECHNIQUES AND TACTICS

STEVE BADDELEY

WITH RICHARD EATON

STANLEY PAUL

NDON

Stanley Paul & Co. Ltd

An imprint of Random House UK Limited

20 Vauxhall Bridge Road, London SW1V 2SA

Random Century Australia (Pty) Ltd
20 Alfred Street, Milsons Point, Sydney 2061

Random Century New Zealand Limited
18 Poland Road, Glenfield, Auckland 10

Century Hutchinson South Africa (Pty) Ltd
PO Box 337, Bergvlei 2012, South Africa

First published as *Badminton in Action* 1988

This expanded edition 1991

Set in Garamond Light by SX Composing Ltd, Rayleigh, Essex

Printed and bound in Great Britain by Clays Ltd

A catalogue record for this book is available from the British Library

ISBN 0 09 177208 7

CONTENTS

ACKNOWLEDGEMENT

Thanks are due to Mary Eaton, Deirdre, Bill and Barbara Baddeley, without whom this manuscript could not have been produced.

The authors and publishers would like to thank photographer Peter Dazeley for the instructional photographs, Louis Ross and Peter Richardson for the use of their copyright photographs, and Anne Gibson for helping to demonstrate the shots.

PREFACE

I shall never forget the day Steve Baddeley turned ten thousand people's emotions. That was in May 1984, in the giant saucer of the Stadium Negara in Kuala Lumpur – where degrees of heat competed with decibels of noise for possession of the senses, and where most of Malaysia expected sticky revenge to be enacted upon England for a Thomas Cup defeat two years previously.

Baddeley was first into the furnace. He was pitched in against Misbun Sidek, a man with a reputation for a dangerously devious wrist, outlandish hair styles, and frighteningly steep angles on his overheads. He was one of the world's top six players and had one of the world's most formidable crowds behind him.

Forty minutes later that crowd had turned from partisan support to booing dismissal of its man. Not that Misbun had disgraced himself. He had simply been beaten by an opponent with brains, bravery and a big smash.

These are a long way from being Steve Baddeley's only assets, but he has used the three qualities more than any others to have contests played to his own strengths. By doing so on this memorable occasion he transformed the mood both of a match and of an entire Thomas Cup tie.

The crowd continued to be critical after that, and Misbun was given a hard time again when he reappeared for the doubles. England went on to win 3–2. They also went on to win the bronze medal. It is the finest achievement they have ever managed, or are ever likely to. Baddeley's famous victory helped trigger it off.

Since then he has gone on to win the European Championships and Commonwealth Games gold medal, taken two World Grand Prix titles, the Indian and the Scottish and finished third in the Grand Prix points table. He has also become the first Englishman since the war to reach the semifinals of the All-England Championships at

Wembley and is most capped English international with 143 caps. In the process he has developed into a man of many parts.

For instance, before winning the vital match that took him to the last four at Wembley, Steve interrupted his preparation to go through the nerve-testing experience of making a speech at a formal luncheon of officials and celebrities. He didn't have to, but he wanted to register his thanks for being given the Badminton Writers' annual award. For that he made many friends. Steve Baddeley may be successful but he is not selfish.

He has also been an occasional journalist, taken a keen interest in politics, been a leading light in the Players' Association, became National Director of Coaching and Development in Scotland, and also one of badminton's best known personalities.

Increasingly, too, he has become one of its best analysts. There could be few better with whom to attempt a book such as this.

RICHARD EATON

Richard Eaton, racket sports correspondent of *The Sunday Times,* also writes on badminton for *The Times* and has travelled more than forty countries covering events. He is a regular contributor to the BBC World Service, a television commentator on badminton, and Editorial Advisor to *World Badminton,* the official magazine of the International Badminton Federation. He has been author or co-author of ten racket sports books including (on badminton) *Playing For Life,* and *Badminton in Action* (also with Steve Baddeley).

CHAPTER 1

THE GAME

The movements of a shuttlecock are amongst the most pleasing sights in sport: flat and fast like the cone of a space capsule in orbit, then slowing and turning like a small parachute in a gravity-resistant eclipse as it descends to earth. The contrasts it creates are unique. Length, width, and height are all important in what is the most three-dimensional of all racket games. A slow-exposure photograph of a shuttlecock over the course of a few rallies would reveal the most ornate and intricate of patterns and parabolas, as though some hidden design of beauty lay behind it all.

Perhaps it does. There is an ancient mystery about the true origins of badminton. Versions of the game have been depicted on pottery that appeared around 3,000 years ago in China. There is evidence of it in ancient Greece, and at about the same time in Japan, India, and Siam. There are medieval woodcuts of shuttles being hit with bats in England.

It is certain, however, that in English country houses during the mid-nineteenth century battledores were used to hit shuttles. Army officers who learnt the game in India played it at Badminton Hall, on the Duke of Beaufort's country estate in Gloucestershire. From this, in 1869, badminton took its name.

Since then, badminton's progress has been so steady that it has become a big sport in three continents and is continuing to make headway throughout the rest of the world. This is not surprising. The action of hitting a delicately feathered piece of cork is intrinsically pleasurable. The way in which it slows is both aesthetically pleasing, and enables the beginner to attain a degree of grace and dignity during those worrying early attempts.

This unique characteristic also makes for disguise and tactical complexities that are richly rewarding for the player who improves. Improvement to the highest level provides an intensely demanding test of stamina and skill and of brain, making it a form of physical chess.

These are the qualities that have attracted players and spectators in very large numbers. There are an estimated four million people playing in England, and 20,000 watched the World Championships in Beijing in 1987. Since going open in 1979, badminton has developed a lucrative World Grand Prix circuit, and the stimulus of having been included in the Olympics in 1992 was enormous.

In a local sports or community centre you are almost certain to find badminton courts. Start with a friend, or ask someone to help you. It is wise to have a little coaching, both for immediate enjoyment and to improve your standard. The club or sports centre should help you obtain it.

The value of coaching is that it develops good habits. Many people stand still and hit to their opponent instead of seeking ways of making opponents move. It is important to take an overhead shot rather than hit it underarm, as many beginners do. For a good length or a powerful smash you need a sound technique.

But remember, many things work that cannot be found in this or any other coaching manual. We hope to reinforce the basics and help you find short cuts, but there is no one way to do things. The advice given here is, we believe, useful. But don't be a slave to it. Advice, knowledge, and technique are good servants but bad masters.

EQUIPMENT

Rackets

Since the early 1980s there has been a racket revolution, and wooden rackets have all but disappeared. There are, to date, three new types of racket: steel, aluminium, and graphite. (Graphite is sometimes mixed with compounds like kevlar or boron.) These materials are lighter, stronger, and faster through the air, so you can hit the shuttle harder and the rackets will last longer. In the early 1990s racket head shapes also diversified. You can now get them in ovals, teardrops and five-sided shapes.

Choose the size of the handle of the racket carefully, according to what feels comfortable. The normal grip size is 3½ or 3⅝ in. The grip size is important. Too small and it may make a player squeeze too tight. That can cause arm trouble. Usually the fingers will come round the handle so that they almost touch the palm.

The balance of rackets varies, so it will help your play if you become aware of the effects of head-heavy or head-light rackets. The better you get, the more you may want to experiment. There is a large choice of good-quality rackets, but it is not necessary to buy from the top end of the range to start with.

Strings

Good, tight stringing is important. Gut strings give more feel and sensitivity, but they are more expensive, so consider them only when you get to a reasonable standard. Meanwhile, the feel of a really tight synthetic racket will compare quite favourably with gut. An increasing number of top players use synthetic strings because of their reliability and because they can be strung extremely tight.

Shuttles

Feather shuttles have a better 'feel' than plastic shuttles. This helps a player develop touch and control, but they are more expensive than plastic shuttles and will not last as long.

For a beginner plastic shuttles are adequate, but if you are good it is better to use feathers. Clubs vary; some use plastic, but many still use feathers.

Weights of shuttles vary a little and can be tested by striking them from the back of the court. They should land around the doubles service line. The rule says a shuttle is of the right pace when, hit by a player with a full underhand stroke, it falls not less than 1 ft 9 in (530 mm) and not more than 3 ft 3 in (990 mm) short of the other back boundary line. Occasionally the test area will be indicated by two small marks. (See diagram I.)

Remember not to store feather shuttles near heat. The natural oils in the feathers can dry up, and then will break easily; so keep shuttles somewhere cool, like a garage. A feather shuttle is a delicate piece of workmanship – don't abuse it. Pick it up gently from the floor; don't crush it by carelessly scooping it up.

Clothes

When choosing clothes, comfort is the main objective. There's nothing worse than a shirt that is tight under the armpits, or shorts that don't allow you to bend properly. Be certain that shorts feel comfortable in the lunging position and that your shirt does not restrict you in the overhead hitting posi-

tion. Many women prefer to wear a skirt (or shorts) and a top, rather than a dress. Use padded socks to help avoid blisters.

Clothing can be prevented from becoming crumpled by using a racket-sized holdall. If you get a holdall, get a racket cover too: damp kit alongside a racket can damage the strings. A plastic bag is useful for damp kit and towels.

Shoes

There are a host of different badminton shoes these days. It is best if the soles have a good grip. Shock absorption is important, as badminton is a very physical game. Whatever you buy, comfort is vital. Don't tie the laces too tightly, as this can cause bruising.

When you have finished playing, always keep warm. Wearing a tracksuit is the best way to do this. It lessens the chances of aches and pains from stiffness.

Grips

Grips are made of leather, towelling, or synthetics. The advantage of towelling is that it can quickly be changed, and it gives a comfortable grip less likely to cause blisters. Leather is more expensive and difficult to change, but hard-wearing.

When you have your equipment, book a court at your local sports or community centre or club for half an hour. Don't overdo it to begin with by playing for too long.

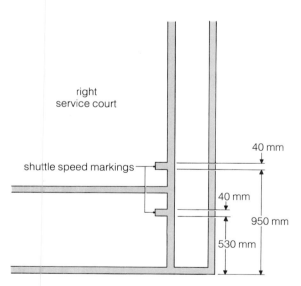

Diagram I. Shuttles of the correct speed should land between the marks each side of the back service line

USING THE FOREARM

It is usually accepted that the first thing you have to learn is how to hold the racket. Well, we are going to be a little bit different. By first acquiring an awareness of how a shuttlecock is hit, the importance of learning the correct forehand grip can be better understood.

It is often said that badminton is a game where the wrist is important. In fact, the wrist has probably been over-rated. Biomechanical study of the overhead shots shows that the wrist actually plays only a minor role. The main source of power is an inward rotation of the upper arm on the forehand, called **pronation** of the forearm; and an outward rotation of the upper arm on the backhand, called **supination** of the forearm.

Don't be frightened off by the scientific-sounding terms. Crudely put, they mean that the forearm twists. This is more important than what you do with the wrist. It also means that if you get this right, you will get the grip right.

Pronation is simply the movement of the forearm turning from inside to out. It's a turning action of the forearm in an anti-clockwise (right-hander), or clockwise (left-hander), direction. The palm ends up facing downwards (see diagram II).

Supination is twisting the other way, for the backhand. The rotation of the forearm is now clockwise for right-handers and anti-clockwise for left-handers (see diagram III). Try doing shadow exercises with and without the racket.

Use the forearm properly, and there is a greater likelihood that you will adopt the correct grip. The reverse is equally true. If you adopt the correct grip, you will have to rotate the forearm in order to hit the shuttle straight (see next section).

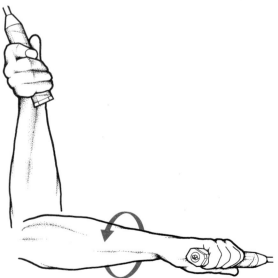

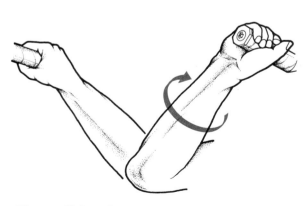

Diagram II. Pronation

Diagram III. Supination

GRIPS AND STANCE

The advice in the following pages assumes the reader to be right-handed. If (like Steve Baddeley) you are left-handed, simply read right for left and vice versa. Some of the photographs do in fact show left-handed players.

Many beginners pick up the racket in a pan-handle grip (see figure 1). The racket face is square to the body and the tendency is to hit with the wrist, which means there will be little power. The best you can manage is a short jabbing action.

To get power you need to pronate the forearm as described. Pick up the racket in the panhandle grip and pronate the forearm in a slow-motion overhead forehand. Can you see what will happen?

The racket face strikes the shuttle out to the right, whereas it needs to go in a straight line (see diagrams IV and V). So we need to establish a grip that allows the racket face to be square to the shuttle after the forearm has been pronated. This is the multi-purpose grip.

Figures 1a-b

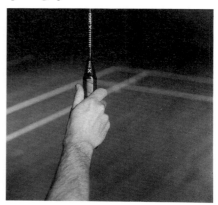

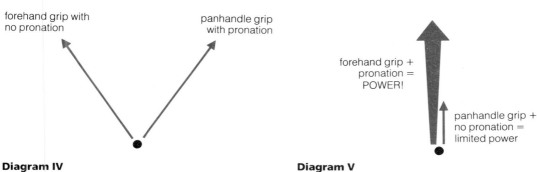

forehand grip with
no pronation

panhandle grip
with pronation

forehand grip +
pronation =
POWER!

panhandle grip +
no pronation =
limited power

Diagram IV

Diagram V

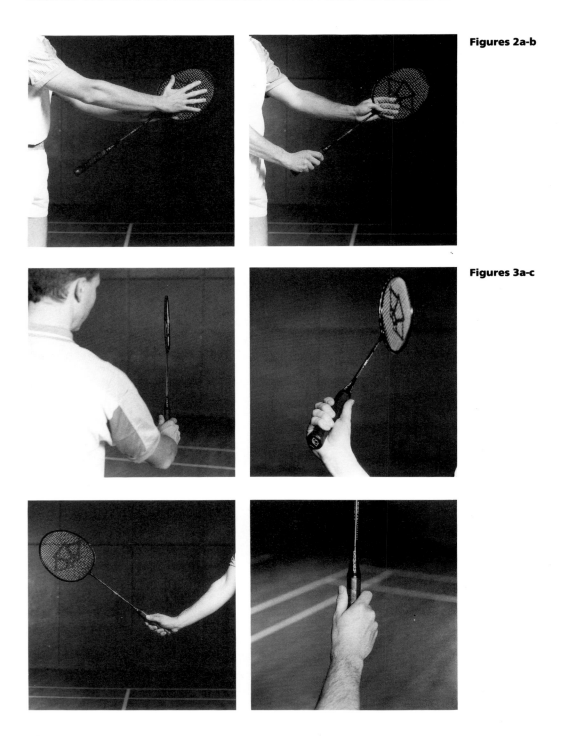

Figures 2a-b

Figures 3a-c

Multi-purpose grip

Here's how to find it. Hold the throat of the racket in the left hand with the racket head perpendicular to the floor. Place the palm of your right hand flat on the strings (see figure 2a).

Slide it down and shake hands with the handle (see figure 2b). Look at the photos (figures 3a to d) which show this grip from a variety of angles. Notice the 'V' between forefinger and thumb (in figure 3d) which rests on the narrower side of the racket handle (see diagram VI). The exact position of this 'V' can vary from player to player; figure 3d shows the 'V' in a classic multi-purpose grip, slightly to the left; it can be in different positions, and if the 'V' were more to the right it would be in the traditional forehand grip position. In recent years the multi-purpose grip has become more popular, although we will call it 'forehand grip' throughout the book because it is used for the overwhelming majority of forehand strokes.

Now try the forehand overhead again. To hit the shuttle straight you must pronate the forearm. If you don't, the shuttle will go sailing off to the left (as in diagram IV)! If the forearm doesn't turn, the racket cannot connect square on to the shuttle.

It is very important to develop a relaxed grip

Diagram VII

with the handle held in the fingers rather than the palm. Check this by adopting your normal grip and then seeing if you can remove your palm from the handle. You should be able to do this and find the racket is still held securely by the fingers as indicated in diagram VII. A common fault is to grip the racket much too tensely which prevents the forearm muscles from working effectively.

The importance of holding the racket lightly becomes obvious when you switch grips. You will sometimes need to switch when playing a backhand. Let's see how.

Backhand grip

Holding the forehand grip, twist the racket slightly in a clockwise direction (as viewed from the player's perspective), using your non-racket hand. The racket turns in your right hand about one-eighth of the handle's circumference – until your thumb is resting along the flat part of the handle (see figures 4a and 4b). Practise changing from one grip to the other, to become as quick and dexterous as possible. However, don't use the non-racket hand. It is only used as a teaching aid to discover the grips. After that, change grips with the fingers of the racket hand.

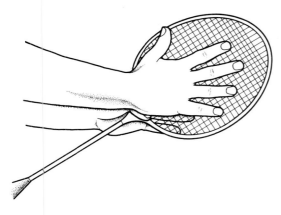

Diagram VI

Figure 4a

Figure 4b

Figure 5 Steve Baddeley in the ready position; also shows the 'base' position, locating the player in relation to the court

Panhandle grip

Next learn the panhandle grip. It can profitably be used around the net area, for kills and pushes, especially in doubles. The palm of the hand is more or less parallel to the flatter side of the handle – like holding a frying pan.

Using the grips

Players at top level use a whole variety of grips. Some use an extreme forehand grip with more palm behind it for forehand shots, switching to the backhand where necessary. Others prefer a multi-purpose grip somewhere closer to the backhand than the classic forearm grip. Then the grip change is minimal. It is vital not to use the panhandle for basic strokes or you will always be limited. The important point is to learn the relationship between the grip you are using and the angle of the racket face.

Ready position

Between shots in a rally, the racket is best held in a relaxed forehand grip, not committed to either side, with the racket hand around waist height (see Zhao Jianhua in photo 1). Many doubles players wait using the backhand grip when in a defensive position.

The racket head position should be variable. If you are expecting a smash or a downward shot, you are more likely to have the racket lower. If the opponent is taking the shuttle below net height you will probably have it higher.

A player needs to be alert and ready to spring swiftly to any area. So the knees need to be bent and the weight on the balls of the feet. The eyes should be fixed on the opponent, his racket, and the shuttle.

Photo 1 Zhao Jianhua, the 1991 World champion from China, in the ready position, with legs bent, eyes on the shuttle, racket just above waist height

The base

COACHING TIPS

BOX 1 **READY POSITION**

1. Head and body upright looking at shuttle.
2. Racket alert; angle at wrist between hand and forearm.
3. Knees slightly bent.
4. Weight on balls of feet, not heels.

In singles you need to reach any area quickly, so try to adopt a fairly central base position. That will be roughly 3 ft (1 m) behind the service line, along the middle line. It isn't fixed; different styles of players have different bases. Also, it will vary depending on what sort of player your opponent is and the state of the rally. If the shuttle is around the net area, the base has to be closer to the net. If a smash is expected, move the base back.

Try to avoid shots that may leave you unable to regain base – unless you are pretty certain of making a winner. Note that it is easier to move forward, but you may find you have less time because the shuttle will usually be coming down faster. It is harder to move backwards, but you have more time. So if you are central, that is about the right position for the base.

Finally, it is best to face the area of the court from which the shuttle will come. If an opponent is hitting from his or her deep backhand side, you should not stand square to the net but move to face it at a slight angle, and directly towards the shot that is coming.

5

FOREHAND OVERHEAD SHOTS

It is worth looking in detail at the overhead forehand, because the technique for this is the same for clears, drops, and smashes. Get this right, and you probably have 40 per cent of the game. Carefully shadow the following moves step by step. It will pay off.

Begin with a forehand grip in the relaxed but alert ready position. As the shuttle sails to the baseline, move backwards with small, light, bouncing steps until you are behind it. Don't turn your back on the net as you do this. You can face forward and still maintain balance and rhythm as you move.

The preparation

The right hand is moved up close to the right shoulder. This brings the racket into the preparatory position. The racket head can be held at head height (see photo 2 of Liem Swie King). A useful tip is to point the racket towards the shuttle. This is a very important coaching idea which can be applied to the preparatory phase of most shots.

The last step must be with the right foot, so that it is further back in the court than the left foot. Then you are sideways to the net with the left shoulder leading. The left hand and arm, like the racket, point up towards the approaching shuttle. This improves balance and helps to ensure that the upper body has turned sideways.

Preparation is now complete. This position can be held until you are ready to commence hitting.

Photo 2 Liem Swie King of Indonesia, three times All-England champion, in a classic forehand overhead preparation position

Hitting

The hitting action is a kind of throwing motion. Think about throwing the racket at the shuttle, similar to the way in which a ball is thrown over-arm.

Practise throwing a shuttle from behind the baseline with both feet stationary, and try to get it over the net. If you are to achieve this you need to develop a correct and powerful throwing action. Then try the same thing, allowing yourself to step forward over the baseline as you throw. Because you are now involving your body weight you should be able to throw the shuttle further. The same principles are used while making an overhead shot.

The hitting phase commences with the racket head being taken back to a position behind the shoulder, or slightly lower. During this movement

Photo 3 Morten Frost of Denmark, four times All-England champion, doing a forehand overhead with the forearm starting to turn

Figures 6a & 6b Notice that in 6a you see the back of the hand and in 6b the front of the hand

the forearm actually supinates and the racket head points directly backwards. Morten Frost shows this well in photo 3.

Once you have started the hitting motion, maintain a continuous movement of the racket. Don't wait with the racket behind the head. Contact is made high above the head with an almost straight arm (see photos 4 and 5 of Morten Frost and Sze Yu).

Remember that the forearm must twist inwards (pronate) to develop maximum power and to hit the shuttle straight. Compare photos 3 and 4 and figures 6a and 6b. For Morten's racket to be square at impact, the forearm must rotate between the position in 3 and impact point shown in 4. The extent of the rotation is increased by the supination enacted when the racket is taken back behind the shoulders (figure 6a).

As the racket swings, the right foot begins to step forward. This ensures that the body weight is transferred forwards, giving more power. It also helps

Photo 4 Frost's overhead this time shows the forearm having turned and the full extension of the arm

Photo 5 Sze Yu of Australia showing the importance of taking the shuttle high and early

the recovery to the base position. Beginners often fail to step forwards and consequently have difficulty getting the shuttle to the other end of the court. At impact, racket head and body should be square to the net as demonstrated by Sze Yu in photo 5.

COACHING TIPS

> ## BOX 2 **OVERHEAD FOREHAND**
>
> **Power**
> - from forearm rotation
> - body rotation
>
> **Preparation**
> - non-racket side of body closer to net
> - non-racket arm pointing to shuttle
> - racket pointing to shuttle
>
> **Impact**
> - body square to net
> - arm straight to take shuttle as high as possible
>
> **Follow through**
> - racket side of body close to net
> - upper body and head kept upright
>
> **N.B.** Racket should flow in continuous loop throughout stroke cycle.

Figure 7
Sequence of eight figures showing forehand overhead technique

Follow-through

The right arm and racket continue forward. On powerful strokes the forearm will continue to pronate after the shuttle has been struck (see photo 6 of Jens-Peter Nierhoff overleaf). The racket shouldn't drop too low on the follow-through as it might impede movement back to base. It is important not to allow the upper body to collapse forward: keep it upright throughout.

The right foot completes its step and the left arm is pulled downwards and backwards past the body. The effect of the right-foot, left-arm movement is to complete the body rotation. The body will now once again be sideways to the net, but this time with the right shoulder leading.

After completing the stroke, the player should use short, light steps to regain the base position.

It is worth remembering that though we have divided this shot into three phases, this should not be shown in the way you hit the shot. You don't want jerky motions like a puppet, but smooth, continuous, flowing movements.

Having mastered the rudiments of this technique it is possible to look in more detail at the variety of overhead shots. Plenty of interesting possibilities are now open to you! By hitting

the shuttle in different overhead positions and with variable force you can play a wide variety of clears, drops and smashes. By using the same basic technique for each you can keep the opponent guessing.

Jump-turn or scissor-kick?

The movement described above involves taking up a side-on position of readiness behind the shuttle and then stepping or jumping forward towards the shuttle. This is ideal when you have plenty of time. It is commonly used when replying to a high singles service, a high defensive clear and a high underarm lift.

If a jump is involved and both feet are off the ground at impact it is called a 'jump-turn'.

However, often a player will be returning attacking shots which do not allow sufficient time either to get behind the shuttle or make a jump-turn. In such cases a movement known as a 'scissor-kick' is used (see diagram VIII overleaf).

The preparation for this is similar to that for a jump-turn in that a side-on position is established with racket and left arm pointing to the shuttle and weight placed on the right foot.

The difference is that, as the right leg propels

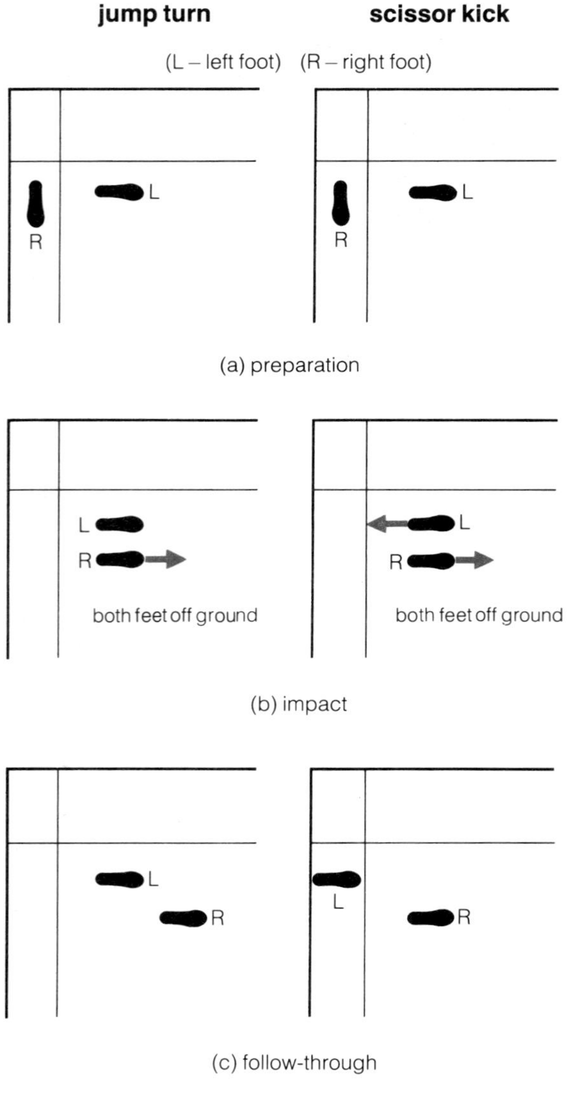

the body into the stroke, the left leg is pulled back. The stroke is played with both feet off the ground (see photo 4 of Morten Frost). The right leg kicks forward during the stroke and landing occurs on the left foot which immediately pushes the body forward to commence movement back to base.

Practise this by standing side-on to the net. Jump so that your feet positions are interchanged. This simple movement is the essence of the scissor-kick. As you become familiar with this movement, gradually make it more dynamic. Soon you will be able to move backwards from base, scissor-kick and return to base. When you feel comfortable with this, introduce a shuttle into the exercise and, starting with single hits, develop towards a continuous clearing rally.

jump turn   **scissor kick**

(L – left foot)   (R – right foot)

(a) preparation

both feet off ground   both feet off ground

(b) impact

(c) follow-through

Diagram VIII

Photo 6 Jens-Peter Nierhoff of Denmark shows full pronation on the follow-through of a powerful overhead smash (compare with photo 3 where you see the heel of the wrist: here you see the back of the hand)

6

CLEARS

These are used to send the shuttle to the back of the opponent's court so that it drops straight down close to the back line.

To achieve this, contact with the shuttle is made slightly behind the head, or immediately above it. The technique of hitting is exactly as described in the previous chapter.

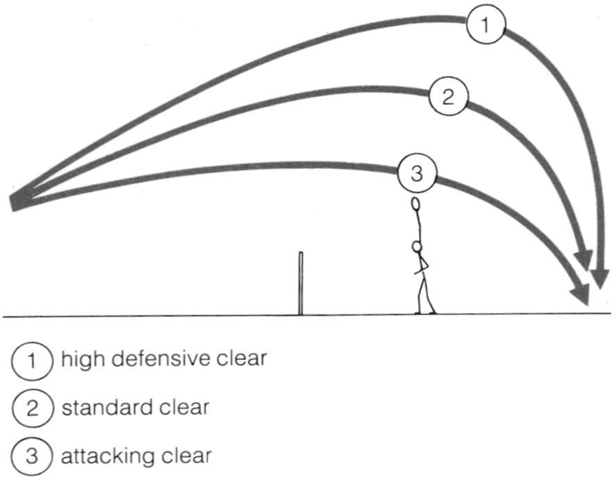

1 high defensive clear

2 standard clear

3 attacking clear

Diagram IX

The high defensive clear

This is a defensive stroke used to allow time to regain a balanced base position at a comfortable pace. It also makes it difficult for the opponent to play an attacking shot. There are two reasons for this:

1. You have made the opponent move to the rear of the court.
2. It is harder to smash a shuttle that is dropping than one travelling in a flatter arc.

The attacking clear

This has a flatter, faster path. Ideally, just above your opponent's outstretched racket. To create this, use the same technique as before, but make contact further forward than for the defensive clear. This will usually be slightly forward of the head.

It is reckless to play the attacking clear if you are out of position. There is far less time than with the defensive clear to recover to base position. If the attacking clear is intercepted you could be left for dead. Played well, the shot will force the opponent back, and make him or her take the shuttle lower than (s)he would wish.

CHAPTER 7

DROPS

The steep drop

The aim of the steep drop is to make the shuttle land as close to the net as possible. The point of impact is similar to that of the defensive clear, but instead of following through powerfully, the hitting action is checked so that the shuttle is not struck too hard. However, it is important not to just dab at it; control is maintained by following through smoothly.

This shot is usually referred to as a 'slow drop'. I don't like this term as it conveys the wrong image. However, the shuttle will travel more slowly compared with a fast or sliced drop shot and it is vital, therefore, that this stroke is played with disguise and deception. This is achieved by ensuring the preparation is identical to that of other overhead shots.

The fast drop

The fast drop will travel further into court than the steep drop, landing between the front service line and the mid-court area.

With the same preparation as for the other strokes, the fast drop has an impact point just forward of the head. This sends the shuttle in a sharp downward direction. The racket-head speed must be slower at impact than for the clear (or smash) but need not be checked as for the steep drop.

With practice the fast drop can become very consistent. It need never drop close to the net, so the delicate touch required for the steep drop is not so necessary.

The sliced drop

This is a variation of the fast drop, with the racket head cutting across the base of the shuttle at an angle. There are two major advantages:

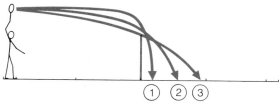

① steep drop
② sliced drop
③ fast drop

Diagram X

1. The shuttle drops shorter, sometimes surprisingly shorter, than a shot hit flat, but the racket-head speed can be fast, suggesting a deeper shot; this is because power is lost on impact, due to the oblique contact.
2. The line of the follow-through of the racket will be different from that of the shuttle, creating deception.

Sometimes the racket-head speed is as fast as that of a smash, in which case the shot may be called a slice smash.

At an advanced level the vast majority of fast drops will be sliced, because they are much more deceptive than ordinarily fast drops. There are two kinds:

Normal slice

The racket slices in a left-to-right direction. Contact is made in front and just to the right of the body (see photo 7 of Ib Frederiksen). The racket head continues towards the camera whilst the shuttle travels in a straight line. You can see the same shot played by a left-hander in photo 8. The greater the slice, the less racket-head speed will be imparted to the shuttle, and the shorter it will fall. This is the most commonly used slice and particularly effective when struck from the forehand side cross-court. This enables it to be hit with a very fast action, yet still land on the short-service line. See from diagram XI how the path of the racket and the path of the shuttle differ.

Reverse slice

The racket slices the shuttle in a right-to-left direction (see photo 9). It is usually played cross-court from the round-the-head position, with contact just to the left of the head. The impact point is frequently above the body or even slightly behind it. Thus it is often hit with the back arching. The forearm must be twisted (pronated) for the racket to impart the glancing blow required. Look at diagram XII.

Photo 7 Ib Frederiksen of Denmark, the 1988 All-England champion, hits an overhead slice straight down the court

Photo 8 (Above right) Steve Baddeley hits an overhead forehand cross-court slice – note the angle of the racket face that has sliced across the base of the shuttle
Photo 9 (Below right) Fiona Smith, the 1990 Commonwealth triple gold medallist, showing the impact of the reverse slice (the racket moves from her right to left)

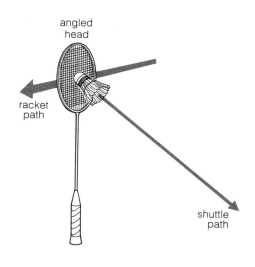

angled
head

racket
path

shuttle
path

Diagram XI

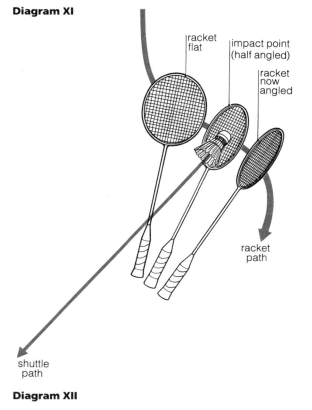

racket
flat

impact point
(half angled)

racket
now
angled

racket
path

shuttle
path

Diagram XII

CHAPTER 8

THE SMASH

The aim of the smash is to hit down fast enough to beat the opponent or force a weak return. This is achieved by a fast racket head at impact and by a flat contact. Slice will lead to loss of shuttle speed. Contact is made in front of the body, as for the fast drops.

Variation, pace and direction are all important. A steep straight smash hit accurately down either sideline is the classic ploy and will reach the floor quickest. Variations include smashing cross-court, straight at the opponent, and a flatter, straight smash into the back tramlines (see diagram XIII).

At a high level it is possible to use a jump smash, popularised by the Far Eastern players. Many of them become airborne before smashing, thus gaining steepness in the trajectory (see photos 10 and 11). However, it is a very tiring shot, and recovery takes longer.

Use of overheads

There is a kind of built-in deception when clear, drop, and smash all look identical in preparation and the opponent doesn't know what's coming. But you can also develop a more deliberate deception: for example, exaggerating the power and tension of the body as though a smash is coming, but producing a drop instead.

Although we have put all these shots into different categories, in reality they exist in a continuum. For example, it is not possible to pin-point exactly where an accurate drop becomes a fast drop and the latter becomes a smash.

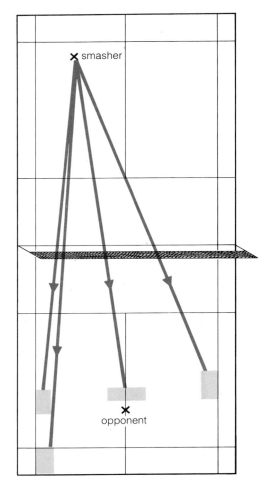

Diagram XIII

Remember, too, that the impact points suggested are only guides. They will vary from player to player and situation to situation.

When you have achieved a basic level of ability, experiment with a variety of shots. Learn to understand the inter-relationship between body position, shuttle position, and racket-head speed and direction. These factors can be juggled to create a profusion of strokes.

Photo 10 Yang Yang of China, the 1987 and 1989 World champion, taking the shuttle early

Photo 11 Zhao Jianhua, the 1991 World champion, getting really high with his spectacular jump smash

9

ROUND-THE-HEAD SHOTS

When the opponent hits the shuttle to the backhand rear corner, you can play a backhand or try to move quickly and play a forehand. Usually the best players try for the latter option. Sometimes the shuttle can be struck directly overhead, but often it is taken to the left of the body (or to the right for a left-hander). When it is, we can easily see why it is called a round-the-head shot (see photo 12).

Look at the sequence of four photos of Anne Gibson, Scotland's number one (figure 8). The shuttle is taken over the left shoulder, which characterises a round-the-head shot. She is square-on throughout the stroke because there is insufficient time to get under the shuttle and make a body turn. After the stroke the weight comes down on to the left leg. Notice too the forearm rotation, which is shown by the changing angles of the racket face.

Such a movement is more tiring than playing a backhand, but it greatly increases power and potential deception. It also enables a reverse slice drop to be played very effectively.

Movement

Move from the base towards the backhand rear corner and if time permits establish a sideways position with the left foot in front of the right. As you make the last step, push off with a jump, hitting the shuttle in mid-air. During the stroke the left foot kicks backward and the right foot forward, so that the left foot lands further back than the right foot (see photo 13 of Icuk Sugiarto). You have transferred your weight as in a normal forehand

Figures 8a, 8b, 8c, 8d Anne Gibson playing a round-the-head stroke

Photo 12 (Right) Steve Baddeley playing a round-the-head clear from the backhand corner – note the position the shuttle is hit in relation to the body

stroke – but in mid-air (see photo 14 of Helen Troke). This is the scissor-kick described previously.

A slight variation to this movement is called the 'Hartono skip' after the great Indonesian champion of the seventies, Rudy Hartono. It can be divided into six major parts. Follow figures 9a to f as you read the text.

Photo 13 (Left) Icuk Sugiarto of Indonesia, the 1983 World champion, doing a scissor-kick whilst executing a round-the-head shot

Photo 14 (Below) Helen Troke, European champion in 1984 and 1986, does a powerful scissor-kick during a reverse slice drop

1. Your starting position is square to the net (9a).
2. Step half a pace backwards with your left foot (9b). This movement characterises the Hartono skip; rotating the body slightly the 'wrong' way gives increased rhythm to the whole movement.
3. Pivot on this foot so that your right foot moves to the rear and you are in a normal overhead preparatory position (9c).
4. Push backwards off your left foot (9d), scissor-kicking.
5. Play a round-the-head stroke as you scissor-kick (9e).
6. Land on your left foot and use your right leg to aid your movement back to base (9f). Also see photo 13 of Sugiarto.

The most natural round-the-head shots tend to be the cross-court reversed slice drops (fast or slow), the straight clear, and the straight smash, which is often extremely powerful.

Figures 9a-f

CHAPTER

10

OVERHEAD BACKHAND SHOTS

No matter how valuable round-the-head shots may prove, don't neglect the backhand. There will always be times when it can be exposed.

Pointers

Backhands can cause problems for players at all levels. It is worth making a few points clear before looking at technique:

1. An overhead backhand requires good timing and technique – not strength.
2. The backhand clear is an impact shot: the follow-through is checked.
3. Do not point the elbow up at the shuttle as you prepare.
4. Unlike the forehand there is no weight transference. You should be able to play a backhand on one leg or standing on a chair. You shouldn't fall off!

The backhand clear

COACHING TIPS

> ### BOX 3 OVERHEAD BACKHAND CLEAR
> **1.** Point racket to shuttle during preparation.
> **2.** No follow-through – impact shot.
> **3.** No transfer of body weight.
> **4.** *Relax*.

Preparation

The right foot steps over the left foot towards the rear of the court, so you have your back to the net. It is not necessary to use the backhand grip. In fact, if the shuttle is between you and the base-line such that you are forced to hit the shuttle from behind you, do *not* use a backhand grip. Such a grip, in this situation will *prevent* you from rotating (supinating) the forearm. Try this out by shadowing a clear behind you with a backhand grip. You should see that if you supinate your forearm, the shuttle will be hit out to the side! A backhand grip is needed when you hit a backhand stroke either in front or to the side of your body. It is of benefit for backhand kills, defence, underarm lifts and drives as we shall see later.

As with the forehand, the racket is pointed towards the shuttle. This is especially important on the overhead backhand as it avoids the common fault of pointing the elbow towards the shuttle during the preparatory phase.

Hitting action

As the stroke begins, take the racket backwards pronating the forearm as you do so. To make this easier, imagine you are wearing a watch and turn your forearm so that you can tell the time. (A good aide-memoire, devised by Scotland premier coach John Williamson, is 'What's the time? Time to play a backhand.')

The racket is now thrown forward, the arm straightens, the forearm rotates (supination) and contact is made as high as possible (see photo 15 of Paul-Erik Hoyer). Ensure that the backward and forward motion of the racket describes a continuous loop throughout the stroke cycle. See the sequence of five images in figure 10.

There is no real follow-through, as you can see in photo 16, in which Darren Hall's backhand is lower than Hoyer's. In fact some follow-through is unavoidable as figure 10e shows. This is because it is not possible to stop a fast moving object dead. However the arm and hand do stop abruptly, and the sensation is of an impact shot. Do not try to transfer body weight into the shot. Often the right foot makes contact with the floor as you make contact with the shuttle.

Pointing the racket at the shuttle during preparation ensures a full-stroke is played and enables you to generate racket-head speed, thus imparting power. You need to be very strong indeed to achieve sufficient power if you start with your elbow up. Think about the forehand stroke. If you start with the racket behind your head and your elbow pointing to the shuttle, you won't be able to generate as much power as with a full stroke. It is the same on the backhand. Starting with the elbow up means you are starting half-way through the stroke.

Figures 10a-e

37

Photo 15 Paul-Erik Hoyer of Denmark, 1992 European champion, reaching to take an early, high overhead backhand

Photo 16 Darren Hall, European champion in 1988, has little follow-through on his backhand

The drop shot

To gain deception, the preparation for the drop shot must be identical to that for the clear. At the last moment the racket-head speed is checked so that the shuttle is not hit too hard. Control is gained by following through smoothly, as with the forehand drop (look at the sequence in figures 11a to c). Continue the follow-through movement and use this to commence the recovery to base.

A word of warning: the backhand overhead drop should be hit fairly fast because opponents will be looking for a weak return. Too slow a drop may enable an enterprising opponent to come in and make a kill.

At an advanced level, the backhand drop is hit by cutting round the outside of the shuttle, contacting both base and skirt and thus gaining greater control.

The smash

Using the same technique as for the clear, strike the shuttle in a downward direction by bringing the wrist right over at impact. The follow-through is checked.

If you don't have great success with this shot don't worry too much about it, as even very good players find it difficult.

Figures 11a-c

The Danish swipe

This is not a shot to be advocated, but it can get you out of trouble as a kind of drive-cum-clear when the shuttle is in the backhand corner. It is sometimes effective for club players who cannot play the overhead backhand.

It is played by moving towards the backhand corner and waiting for the shuttle to drop below shoulder height. Move the right foot into the shuttle, point the elbow, and sweep the arm into the shot, following through strongly. It is a powerful shot: the body goes forward and there is quite a bit of swinging forward and twisting into it. Hit it hard and high, to increase the chance of recovering to a reasonable position, or drive it fast and flat to pressurise the opponent. If you find it effective, use it in matches and practise the overhead technique at other times.

NET SHOTS

Many matches are won and lost at the net. In singles an opponent can be tied up at the net and frustrated. Baddeley's best battles have often been won that way! The essence of creative net shots is delicacy and touch, and in winning net shots, speed and anticipation.

Movement on the forehand

There are three main ways of moving from the base to the net – two types of stepping and a chassé. All end with a lunge to reach the net quickly whilst balanced.

Figures 12a-d

Step

In this movement the non-racket leg steps in front of the leading foot, followed by a lunge on to the racket leg – as shown in the sequence in figures 12a to d.

net

base position

lunge

Diagram XIV

Figures 13a-d

Chassé

Here one leg is drawn up to the other, but does not pass or step behind it. The leading leg then continues in a lunge (see figures 13a to d).

Diagram XV

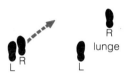

net

base position

Figures 14a-d

Step behind

Here the trailing leg is pulled across and behind the leading leg, creating a push-off for a lunge by the leading leg to the net (see figures 14a to d). Although this movement appears awkward, it is commonly used. The apparently uncomfortable intermediary position creates a springboard to propel the body.

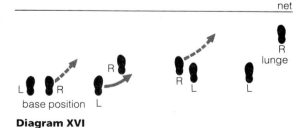

net

base position

Diagram XVI

41

Use any of these for moving from base to the net. Most players will use all three movements at different times. It is vital that the final step, the lunge, which often covers much ground, is with the right foot – for right-handers (see photo 17).

Photo 17 Darren Hall moves swiftly, lunging on his racket leg to play a backhand with a backhand grip

Movement on the backhand

There are two principle ways of moving from base to the net on the backhand side.

Step

This is similar to the step movement on the forehand net. In figures 15a to c look at how Anne Gibson moves on to her left leg and then lunges on her right.

The different forehand movements are shown in three diagrams XIV, XV, XVI.

Figures 15a-c

Chassé

As you see from figures 16a to c, the first movement involves turning so that the right side of the body faces the backhand front corner. The left leg is then drawn up close to the right, from which position the body is propelled forward.

Figures 16a-c

Stroke and recovery

It is essential to take the shuttle as high as possible, ideally at tape height. (If you meet the shuttle higher than that you will probably be attempting a kill, see p.46.) The arm will be outstretched and the racket should move in the simplest possible line from the body.

Balance is vital and at the moment of impact, there should be what I call 'a moment of calm' as perfect balance and control is obtained whilst the shuttle is played delicately over the net.

To recover, bring your left leg part way towards your right and push off your right leg back to base.

Photo 18 (Above) Steve Baddeley takes a high early net shot against Morten Frost

Photo 19 (Right) Michael Kjeldsen, an All-England doubles finalist, playing a net shot off the racket leg with a backhand grip

The racket shouldn't drop; simply pull it in towards your body, once the shot is completed keep it around waist or chest height as you move back. Your head and upper body should be steady at impact and mustn't collapse forward. To prevent this happening you need strong stomach and back muscles. Look at photos 18–19: both players demonstrate good balance and concentration as the net shot is played.

COACHING TIPS

> ## BOX 4 **NET SHOTS**
> **1.** Racket should travel in simple path straight to shuttle.
> **2.** Good lunge is important — requires leg strength *and* flexibility.
> **3.** 'Moment of calm' at impact: head and body still.
> **4.** Small gentle hitting action.
> **5.** Don't let racket drop or body collapse after impact.

Hitting

The principles are the same on both backhand and forehand. A net shot requires a very short back-swing and follow-through. It is a very delicate, gentle stroke. Since you don't need power, grips can vary. Don't let the shuttle passively bounce off the strings. Caress it over, close to the tape.

When players start, they sometimes jab at the shuttle from below. Try to avoid this by developing a delicate touch. There is a great contrast: you come in very powerfully and then need to use a gentle touch. It's all done together – so it is a testing combination to achieve. That is one of the beauties of badminton.

Delicacy is aided by a light grip, as it is a combined movement of hand, wrist, and fingers that produces the control. You can make very large and rapid improvements in your touch and control through practice.

It is important with net shots to experiment, and there is plenty of scope for individualism. Remember: in singles the vital but difficult thing is to get to the shuttle early. The earlier you reach the shuttle, the easier it is to play an effective net shot.

Net shots can be played without deception when a player gets there quickly, believing he has reached it early enough not to be threatened. More often, however, you will want to shape for an alternative shot. That usually means threatening a flick shot over your opponent's head (see pages 50 and 51).

Spins

As you meet the base of the shuttle it is simple to impart a slight spin, or turn, with a brushing action (see photo 19 of Michael Kjeldsen). Using your wrist, cut across the base, in either direction. It is easier from right to left on the forehand, and from left to right on the backhand. The idea is to make the shuttle turn over, so that as it crosses the net the cork will not always be presented to the opponent's racket. If he tries to hit the feathers he will have very little control.

Hairpins

If the shuttle has dropped low, spins are usually too hazardous. Instead it has to be returned in a trajectory that forms a hairpin. The shuttle crosses the net and descends very steeply the other side. This shot requires delicacy of touch, as it must lose pace and start to come down just above tape height.

Kills

If you take the shuttle above the tape, hit it down and try to make a winning shot. Move as you would to the other net shots, although a little more explosively to take the shuttle slightly higher.

On the forehand side use the normal forehand grip, or the panhandle grip if you prefer. On the backhand you need the classic backhand grip (see photo 20 of Jan-Eric Antonsson) with the thumb along the flat part of the handle so that it can control the racket head.

The kill shot is an impact shot for three reasons. Firstly, you can generate plenty of power without

Figures 17a-d

following through. Secondly, you might hit the net and be faulted if you do follow through. Finally, you need to keep your racket up ready for any return.

As you move in, point the racket towards the shuttle, take it back to around head height and then swiftly forward hitting the shuttle sharply downward with a short tapping action. After impact, ensure your racket is kept high and be alert for any returns.

Look at figures 17a to d: notice how the head and body are kept up throughout the stroke so that there is no tendency to collapse with the shot. Normally the shot is played either before the leading foot lands, or as it lands.

Notice in sequence 18a to c, in which Anne Gibson is showing the backhand kill, how she has shortened her grip to gain more control. It is well worth experimenting with shortened grips on both forehand and backhand sides. Simply hold the handle further up so that your first finger is close to the plastic bevel.

Figures 18a-c

Photo 20 Jan-Eric Antonsson of Sweden trying a backhand kill – note the grip with the thumb behind the handle

Photo 21 (Right) Sze Yu about to play a forehand kill

CHAPTER 12

LIFTS FROM THE FORECOURT

Photo 22 Morten Frost playing a
forehand flick against Icuk Sugiarto — notice Morten's
forearm muscles

The flick

If you learn the flick as an alternative to a net shot, you will have the options of playing the shuttle delicately over the net, or flicking it with a fast, short action to the back.

The perfect flick will travel just over the outstretched racket of your opponent so that it can't be intercepted. However, occasionally you may be able to push it past, rather than over, your opponent on a flatter path, especially if (s)he is moving in rapidly, expecting a net shot.

The flick shot is played with a short backswing and minimal follow-through. Power is generated rapidly by using forearm rotation (see photo 22). The preparation must copy that for a net shot with the stroke-cycle being delayed to the last possible moment. The racket is moved rapidly away from the shuttle – the backswing – and immediately towards it again to send the shuttle hurrying to the rear of the opponent's court. A backhand flick will require a backhand grip and you should feel your thumb working as the shot is executed.

Photo 23 Steve Baddeley plays a backhand flick over Jens-Peter Nierhoff – notice he has not used a backhand grip!

The high lift

There is an important distinction between the flick and the high lift. Whereas the flick is a threatening shot, the high lift from the net is defensive, particularly when played from halfway down the net or lower. From this position a net shot is still possible, but a flick is difficult because of the lack of angle to play with. When you take the shuttle very low you will need quite a lot of power to get it to the back. This can only be achieved with a larger swing.

The actions of the lift and the flick may be similar but the effect is different. Because the lift goes high it will drop straight down at the back of the court (see diagram XVII). The flick goes flatter and faster, in more of a parabola.

With the high lift you can extend the backswing to generate more racket-head speed. It doesn't matter that you telegraph your intentions because the shuttle should go too high to be cut off.

As before, use the backhand grip for the backhand and the forehand grip for the forehand. For both backhand and forehand you must come in on the right leg. If you don't, you will lose distance and balance.

Remember, too, that you should create adequate recovery time with the high lift, but after the flick you can be vulnerable. If your opponent reads it and intercepts it you may be caught out of position. That is in the nature of any fast attacking shot. So think carefully about when to flick and when to lift.

Diagram XVII

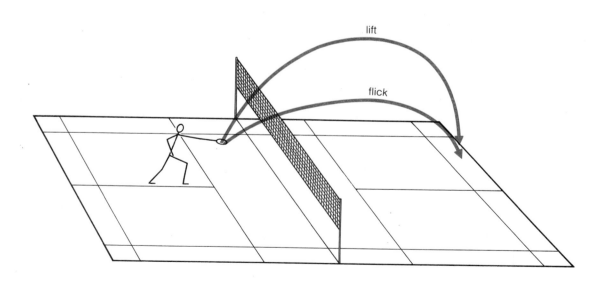

DEFENCE

Plenty of good players base their game on defence and are happiest when the opponent is smashing. They like the shuttle to be hit fast at them, because that may enable them to get their opponent out of position. Defence can create an opportunity to attack.

Even if we do not categorise Morten Frost as a defensive player – perhaps he bases his game more on speed – there are many top players whom we can. The former world no. 1 Xiong Guobao and the 1991 world finalist Allan B. Kusuma both built their games around defence, as did Nick Yates, England's former Japan Open champion.

Defence should be used both to return the shuttle safely and to set up an attack. First, however, learn to return the smash safely.

Photo 24 Helen Troke shows poise and balance as she hurries to return a drop to the forehand

Movement

On the forehand all defensive shots are played off the right foot, which should be pushed rapidly out towards the sideline. Often one step will be adequate, but you may need a chassé first to reach very wide shots. Left-handers, of course, lunge on the left leg, as shown in figures 19a and b.

Figures 19a-b

On the backhand, lunge across where possible with the left foot, and make the return off this leg (see photo 25 of Prakash Padukone). However, it is not always possible to reach a wide smash in this way because the racket has to come across the body, and cannot reach so far. It will often be necessary therefore to take a small sideways step with the left foot and then lunge across with the right (see photo 26 of Nick Yates). The return will be made off the right leg. Recovery is slower from this position, so only use the 'step-over' when really necessary.

Photo 25 (Left) Prakash Padukone, the 1980 All-England champion, plays a backhand defence off his left foot (compare this with Nick Yates' step-over defence in photo 26)

Photo 26 (Above) Nick Yates retrieves a smash wide to his backhand by stepping across with his right foot

Photo 27 Razif Sidek of Malaysia defending, taking the shuttle off his right hip and in front of him (he and his watching brother Jalani won the 1991 World Grand Prix doubles title)

To defend against smashes directed at the body, there are two methods: take the shuttle in front of the body (see photo 27) or move the body out of the way. The latter requires nimble footwork, so that space is created in which to play the return. Usually there is only time to use the first method.

To react quickly enough to return a smash, a good base position and good ready position are vital (see section on grips and stance on p.13). The base position should be flexible. The stronger the attack, the further back you may want to be. Usually it is best to have the racket in front of the body, ready to move to either side.

You often see good players anticipating which side the smash is directed. That is because 'telegraphing' the smash – sending inadvertent messages about where it is going – is common. Anticipate, by all means. But remember: if this policy succeeds once, and you make a penetrating return off your opponent's smash, (s)he may adjust this shot next time.

The block

The block is the defensive shot to learn first. The shuttle is played back to the opponent's front court. From a very powerful smash you may only have time for the shuttle to bounce off the racket over the net. However, when possible try to use a short backswing, as this is more deceptive.

Learn to block straight, then cross-court. In singles, the cross-court block makes it tough for the smasher because (s)he has to go from the back corner to the opposite front corner, the furthest movement. You can either guide the follow-through to caress the shuttle over the net, or impact the shuttle using the angle of the racket face to

create the trajectory. By combining these factors, two types of block can be played.

One is a hairpin block. This is hit slightly upwards, so as to drop close to the net, and perpendicular to it. The other is a flat block, played flatter and faster, to cross just above net height, deeper into the opponent's court.

The advantage of the hairpin is that it brings the opponent right into the net. Its disadvantages are that it is a slower shot – giving the opponent more time to react – and it is harder to play well. If the opponent does reach it early he may kill it or play a tight net shot.

The advantage of the flat block is that, as a faster shot, it is harder for an opponent to reply with a tight net shot. A disadvantage is that it is easier for him to reach. At international level the very tight block would only be employed against a tired opponent, or perhaps one who has smashed off-balance.

The lift

The aim of the lift is to return the shuttle to the rear of the court. It is important to ensure that it goes over the opponent's racket, otherwise it may present an easy opportunity to smash.

Start with the racket in front of the body, pointing roughly towards the shuttle. Take it back and then forward in a continuous loop as with the other strokes we have discussed. The whole action is short but the forward movement must be fast to generate sufficient racket-head speed and to enable the shuttle to be struck to the rear of your opponent's court. The follow-through is minimal and the racket finishes its path by being brought back in front of the body.

You will require appropriate backhand and forehand grips to ensure you use your forearm to full potential.

Even if you find lifting to a length difficult, try not to tense up. As with most strokes it is so important to stay relaxed.

The drive

This is faster and flatter than the lift and although played in a similar way, the angle is different. The shuttle is driven fast and flat at tape height. Once again the stroke cycle is short and timing is very important. As with other defensive shots you are turning the power of your opponent's smash to your advantage.

The drive return is used in doubles off weak smashes to bypass the opposing net player and force the smasher to play a defensive shot.

With all defensive shots relaxation is important. At club level quite a lot of players are leaden-footed, and tense in the arm. If you stay relaxed and alert even the best smashes can be returned effectively.

Photo 28 Morten Frost, on base, perfectly balanced, defending with a forehand block against a smash

CHAPTER 14

SINGLES SERVICE

The demands of the law on serving (see pp.61 and 62) are so stringent that the server usually starts off at a disadvantage. This has been so marked in doubles that it has led to an ongoing debate about whether or not to change the rules.

The receiver's advantage is less clear-cut in singles. He has a longer court to cover, and should be wary about committing himself to a return that leaves him out of position.

The high serve

The aim of the high serve is to move the opponent as far back as possible, making it hard to start an attack. Because it moves him the maximum distance, he will be left out of position if he tries a fast attacking shot.

As well as achieving a good length it is advantageous to hit the shuttle high. This makes it drop almost straight, which is far harder to attack.

Stand about 1 metre from the front line, and close to the middle line. Use the forehand grip for a high serve and (assuming you are a right-hander) stand with your left foot forward so that you are comfortably balanced.

Face towards the diagonally opposite service court and hold the shuttle by the feathers, with the feathers upwards. If it were allowed to drop, it would land to the right of the leading foot, level

with the toes. Let the shuttle fall and strike it just above knee height. The front knee should be relaxed, not stiff; otherwise it tends to lock the buttocks and the back.

The wrist, slightly cocked, is above the elbow as the arm is taken back. When it sweeps down there is a releasing of the wrist just before impact, and, as it becomes an extension of the arm, it locks. There should be a solid feeling when the high serve is struck, and the whole action should be smooth and flowing.

As the shuttle is struck, the body weight comes forward, and there is a slight twisting of the trunk, but the head stays level. The follow-through should be long and high to give the shuttle height and depth. There is plenty of time to establish base position.

A slight transfer of weight during the high serve gives extra power and rhythm. This transfer can be seen in the feet: often the front foot will start with only the heel touching the court. On completion of the shot the back foot is on its toes.

Work through the sequence of eight photographs in figures 20a to h showing Anne Gibson delivering a high singles service.

Aim for the middle of the back line of the service court. There are advantages in serving wide but the risk of error is greater, and to miss a serve in singles is a crime! Depth and height are more important than position along the back line.

Figures 20a-h

The low serve

No matter how good the high serve is, the chances are that it will give the initiative to the opponent. The low service has therefore gained in popularity since the mid-1970s. Now many leading men serve low, some as much as 90 per cent of the time. In women's singles, however, the high serve still dominates.

Take full advantage of the rules, and get the racket well above the knees when you make contact. Relax. You need an action that is very consistent, so that it can be performed under pressure. It should also enable you to flick, to stop opponents anticipating. Therefore try to hold the wrist back, keeping it cocked throughout the stroke. Stay well balanced, don't have too short a preparatory swing, and follow through smoothly. It is neither practical nor necessary to have the same build-up for both the high and the low serve. It does not matter if you telegraph the high serve: the opponent has plenty of time to see it anyway.

The low serve should pass close to the net tape, but don't make mistakes by playing it too tight. In singles, only an opponent of the highest standard will kill the return. Variation, however, is important, and this can be brought about by serving to different positions along the front line, and to different depths.

The laws governing service in badminton

11. SERVICE

11.1 In a correct service:

    11.1.1 neither side shall cause undue delay to the delivery of the service;

    11.1.2 the server and receiver shall stand within diagonally opposite service courts without touching the boundary lines of these service courts; some part of both feet of the server and receiver must remain in contact with the surface of the court in a stationary position until the service is delivered (law 11.4);

    11.1.3 the server's racket shall initially hit the base of the shuttle while the whole of the shuttle is below the server's waist;

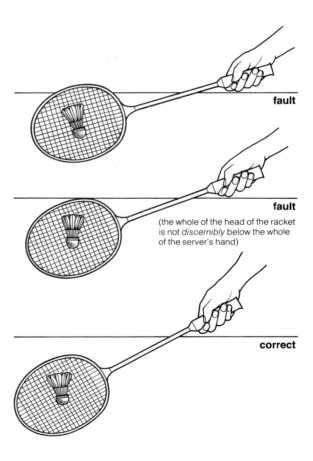

fault

fault

(the whole of the head of the racket is not *discernibly* below the whole of the server's hand)

correct

Diagram XVIII

11.1.4 the shaft of the server's racket at the instant of hitting the shuttle shall be pointing in a downward direction to such an extent that the whole of the head of the racket is discernibly below the whole of the server's hand holding the racket (see diagram XVIII);

11.1.5 the movement of the server's racket must continue forwards after the start of the service (law 11.2) until the service is delivered; and

11.1.6 the flight of the shuttle shall be upwards from the server's racket to pass over the net, so that, if not intercepted, it falls in the receiver's service court.

11.2 Once the players have taken their positions, the first forward movement of the server's racket is the start of the service.

11.3 The server shall not serve before the receiver is ready, but the receiver shall be considered to have been ready if a return of service is attempted.

11.4 The service is delivered when, once started (law 11.2), the shuttle is hit by the server's racket or the shuttle lands on the floor.

11.5 In doubles, the partners may take up any positions which do not unsight the opposing server or receiver.

The flick serve

This should be hit in a flat arc, just high enough so that your opponent cannot reach it, but dropping after it has gone past him. It stops the opponent rushing in fast on the low service, and should have the same technique as the low service, except that the wrist is uncocked at the last moment.

It is illegal to use two actions in the same serve, so it will be unusual for the flick serve to be deceptive enough to be an outright winner. However, a good flick will force opponents to take the shuttle behind them.

Be careful, because a bad flick or a flick correctly anticipated can give the receiver a simple half-court smash. Therefore it must have the same preparation as the low serve.

The backhand serve

This is not a common variation in singles , but it is used by some of the best Indonesians, particularly Icuk Sugiarto. The main disadvantage is that it is difficult to serve a good-length flick with the backhand, which allows the receiver to move up the court to meet the low serve early.

The drive serve

A drive serve is hit fast and flat, often to head height. This can rush the receiver and cause an error. It may also entice the receiver to attack, but usually (s)he will smash back along the same path, which can be anticipated. However, there is quite a large element of risk in using this serve, as a good smash return can sometimes result.

The most effective drive serve is usually done by standing slightly wider than usual in the right-hand court, and driving down the receiver's backhand towards the back centre line. This often leads to a smash back to the server's forehand, which can be anticipated. Beware of the agile opponent who may be able to smash into the open gap left down the server's backhand.

Remember: the essence of good serving is variety. A high serve can go to different altitudes. A low serve can be pushed further and faster so that it doesn't hang over the net. Vary the trajectory, the direction, and the speed. Use all the different serves in varying combinations.

SINGLES TACTICS

It is obvious that you should play to opponents' weaknesses and avoid their strengths. For example, some players are very deceptive around the net; consequently, serving high to them would be a sensible initial tactic. If such an opponent serves low to you, then a deep lift or a flat push to the corners would be the best reply.

Many of your opponents will have weak overhead backhands. To expose this weakness, it is not sufficient just to clear or lift to the backhand corner, as this would usually result in a round-the-head reply. You need firstly to move your opponents out of position – probably drawing them into the front forehand corner – and then play to the rear backhand side so that they have to play a backhand.

A weakness is often considered to be the area in which players make most mistakes. However, it is also worth noticing the area from which they make fewest winners. Commonly this is the rear forehand corner. When in trouble, this will often be a safe place to which to hit (see photo 29, in which the best that Steve Baddeley can do is play to a safe place and thrust back to base as fast as possible).

Think, too, of the overall type of game. Some players like a fast, flat game, full of smashes, fast drops and net play. Others prefer a slower, more controlled game, using the full length and width of the court, with high clears and slow drops. Some like to defend, using the power of the smash by changing its direction and making the attacker work hard to recover from his shot.

What do you do if your best style of play suits the

Photo 29 Steve Baddeley takes a shuttle in a difficult position, low in the forehand corner

opponent's best style? The answer will vary from situation to situation, but where possible it is probably better to play your natural game. It is hard to play in an unfamiliar style when under pressure. However, lack of adaptability can lose you matches.

Sequences

With experience you will learn that patterns or sequences of shots can be repeated many times in matches. This is often because a shot is so effective that it forces the opponent to play a specific return. An excellent example of this occurs when a steep, powerful smash is played close to the sidelines. This can leave the defender time only to get the racket into the path of the shuttle, and this limits the return to a straight block. By anticipating this reply, the attacker can move quickly in towards the net and take the shuttle early, killing the shuttle, or playing an effective spin net shot.

Another example of this idea is as follows. Play a fast clear into your opponent's forehand corner. If you are able to cause the shuttle to be taken from behind or with a bent arm from head height or below (see photo 29), then the usual return, by most players, will be a straight drop. You can anticipate this and gain a commanding position in the rally.

How can you prevent the same thing happening to you? Quite simply, you must learn to play at least two shots from any position on the court. This will help to prevent your opponent from anticipating too early the shot you are about to play.

Imagine you are caught playing the shuttle from deep in your backhand or forehand corners. You may be unable to hit a good clear from this situation, especially on the backhand; the easiest return is a straight drop (as mentioned above), but you should develop a cross-court drop as well. This doesn't have to be played too often – you simply have to let your opponent know that you are capable of an alternative shot, so that the return

cannot be foreseen. You may also be able to develop a powerful drive, using a Danish swipe on the backhand or a kind of squash shot on the forehand.

Cross-court shots

All the shots we have discussed can be hit straight or cross-court. There are several disadvantages of playing cross-court: the shuttle travels further and so gives the opponent more time to react, the striker is left further out of position, and the shuttle passes across the central line and is liable to be intercepted.

However, cross-court shots do have the advantage of making opponents turn, a major weakness in many players. Sometimes players will establish a position on the base which faces the shuttle but closes the body slightly to a cross-court, so increasing the turn they have to make to retrieve a cross-court shot. Cut drops are particularly effective cross-court as they can be played at a steeper angle and so drop closer to the net.

Margin of error

Singles is a game of many factors, two of which to some extent are opposed: consistency and accuracy. When considering these two factors we should think about margin of error. For instance, when hitting a drop or a smash it is silly to aim for the lines, as this will usually result in a large number of errors. Work out your own margin. If you can smash within a foot of a given spot consistently, then aim the shuttle to go a foot inside the sideline. Then your most wayward shot may still land in.

This applies to most shots, though sometimes it will be necessary to take risks to win points.

DOUBLES

Photo 30 Attacking and defensive positions in doubles, with Shuuji Matsuno and Shinji Matsuura of Japan attacking against Michael Kjeldsen and Jens-Peter Nierhoff of Denmark

The doubles game is hugely popular in Britain, and represents many people's experience of badminton. As well as being an extremely sociable form of the game, it is full of variety and entertainment, both in its strokes and its tactics.

The basic techniques on overheads, defence, and net shots are the same for doubles. However, the placements, the frequency of use of each shot, and the tactics are very different. There are two basic formations in doubles: the attacking, in which players adopt front and back positions, and the defending, in which players are roughly side by side (see photo 30). Usually when one partnership is in one of these formations, their opponents should be using the other one.

Men's doubles

Generally speaking, it is better to attack, as you will then be controlling the game. The attacking pair can hit down whilst the defensive pair are forced to lift. Park Joo Bong and Kim Moon Soo of South Korea, the 1991 World champions, and Li Yongbo and Tian Bingyi of China, the 1989 World champions, are both primarily attacking combinations.

Photo 31 Billy Gilliland and Dan Travers, 1986 Commonwealth gold medallists, in doubles serving positions. Gilliland toes the line whilst serving well out in front of the body; Travers has his racket up and legs bent

Women's doubles

Women at international level have reactions comparable to men's, and can defend almost as well as men. However, women do not smash so hard, and so defence can dominate play at the highest level. This is especially noticeable with Chinese and South Korean pairs, resulting in long rallies with little incentive for either pair to attack.

However, this is a development affecting only the very highest levels: in most situations the attacking game will reign supreme.

The serve

Look at the position of the server and the partner in photo 31. The serve should be aimed low, gaining the attack by forcing the opponent to lift.

There are many styles of serving, but you always need to be balanced and to stand close to the 'T'. Too far back and you leave a gap in the forecourt.

Make use of the limits of the laws by making contact with the shuttle as high as legally possible (see

Figures 21a-f

laws on pages 62 and 63). This can be achieved by bending the arm at the elbow, shortening the grip, making contact with the shuttle out to the side of the body, or by combining these factors.

The forehand serve

It is important to have a consistent, smooth action that can be repeated under pressure. Therefore keep it simple.

The essence of good serving is rhythm (see figures 21a to f). There should be a transfer of body weight during the stroke. At the beginning, weight will be on the back foot and it will transfer to the front foot in the course of the stroke. At the end of a service, the back heel should be off the floor. It is important to involve the hips and shoulder in the action. Check that the rear hip swings forward with the service action. The wrist is kept cocked throughout. I feel the sensation is that the heel of the hand leads the stroke.

The placement of the shuttle can be made to any point along the front line. Common targets are to the 'T', and wide, but use the space in between as well. Serve to the receiver's weakest spot: for example, the backhand if the opponent prefers the forehand.

The shuttle should pass over the net as close to the tape as possible. The highest point of its flight should be as it crosses the tape, so that it dips downwards into the opponent's court. Vary the depth. Usually it should land on the front line, but sometimes push it a foot or two into the service box. Also vary the position from which you serve; moving just a few inches away from the middle line can unsettle your opponent by altering the angle of flight.

After the service is complete lift the racket to head height, incorporating this in the follow-through. This enables you to be ready for a return to the net, and intimidates the opponent. Also, make a step towards the net part of your follow-through. This is shown clearly in figure 21f.

The backhand serve

The backhand serve should be struck further in front of the body than the forehand (see photo 31 of Billy Gilliland). Use the backhand grip, which provides enough power to create a variation of the flick serve. Many people find the backhand an easier serve. There is a half-uncocking of the wrist, and the position of the hand usually makes this a comfortable and natural movement. By keeping the elbow up, it is easy to contact the shuttle high. Striking the shuttle from the hand reduces the margin of error. You can strike the shuttle close to the net by 'toeing the line' and leaning forward. This cuts down the reaction time for the receiver. Since the service action is so simple, many players find it quite easy to develop a consistent backhand serve.

COACHING TIPS

BOX 5 **PROCEDURE FOR BACKHAND SERVING**
1. Stand in a comfortable position close to the 'T' (figure 22a).
2. Place racket in the vertical serving position (figure 22b).
3. Place shuttle on strings. (This sequence avoids contravening law 11.2 which refers to the first forward movement of the racket as representing the start of the serve.) Hold shuttle vertically by its skirt and angle it slightly so the cork only is touching the strings. (This avoids contravening law 11.1.3 which states that 'the server's racket shall initially hit the base of the shuttle'.) See figure 22c.
4. Bend arm at elbow (figure 22d).
5. Straighten arm and gently caress shuttle over the net (figures 22e, f and g).

However, the backhand serve does have disadvantages. It takes marginally longer to get the racket up after the serve, and you may need to change to a forehand grip to prepare for the third shot. Also, it is harder to vary the direction of serve along the front line and it is more difficult to develop a good length flick.

Figures 22a-g

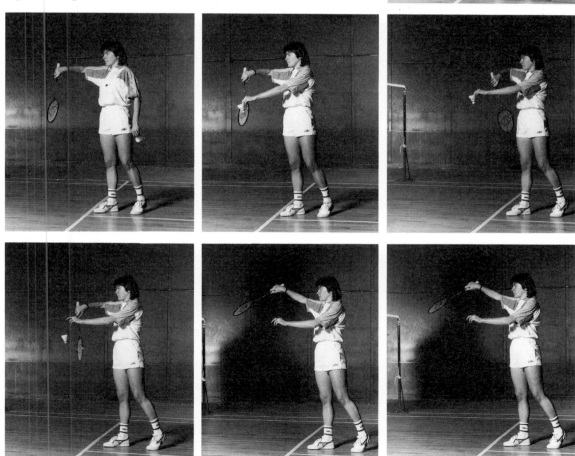

The flick serve

This serve is hit towards the rear of the receiver's court. It should travel in a fast, flat arc but still out of the opponent's reach.

It is important that the preparation for the flick and low serve is identical, unlocking the wrist at the last moment to produce the flick. Make sure the trajectory goes over the opponent. If (s)he cuts it out, it may present an easy smash.

Return of low serve

Look at the serving and receiving positions in photo 32 of Tian Bingyi and Li Yongbo. The return of serve requires great concentration and alertness (see photo 33 of Gill Clark and Gillian Gowers of England). It also requires skill and knowledge. There are four main types of return in doubles:

Photo 32 1989 World doubles champions Tian Bingyi and Li Yongbo of China, and Eddie Hartono and Sutanto Hadibowo of Indonesia, in the classic return of serve and serving positions

Photo 33 (Right) A study in concentration whilst receiving serve: Gillian Gowers and Gill Clark, former European womens doubles champions

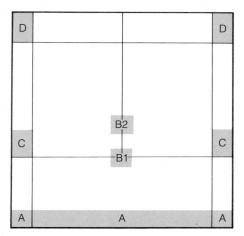

A   tight to net
B1 body of server
B2 body of server's partner
C   midcourt between opponents
D   back corners

Diagram XIX

(a) To the net When this is played straight it is often the easiest way of getting a lift. Hitting the return to the sides is more difficult, but is a useful variation (see diagram XIX).

(b) At the opponents
1. A delicate push can hit the server in the chest as (s)he moves forward. If allowed to land it would fall just beyond the 'T'. It is useful against servers who quickly follow their serve to try to prevent you playing to the net.
2. A harder push at the chest of the server's partner

is effective, but be careful not to push the shuttle out the back or in an upward direction.

(c) To the mid-court A push down either sideline often finds a gap in the mid-court between the opponents.

(d) To the rear-court
1. A flat push to either corner is effective if both opponents are moving up the court to crowd the return.
2. A lift to the corners, which may be negative, but is sometimes necessary – especially if you have started to leave the serve, thinking it may land short.

Whichever return is favoured, it is important to intercept the shuttle as early as possible once it has crossed the net. The best way to do this is to take up an aggressive stance close to the front service line as demonstrated in figure 23a. Naturally, right-handers will have their left leg forward.

Body weight is forward so that there is tension in the leading leg. This enables the front leg to drive the player backwards should a flick be delivered.

If a low serve is struck, push the racket forward in a straight line directly towards the shuttle. The racket side of the body inevitably follows behind the racket resulting in the racket leg stepping forward as in figure 23b. A common fault is to drop the racket and not take it in a straight line to the shuttle.

Figures 23a-b

Tactics

When returning a serve, try and take it early. Hustle a low serve. This is necessary because generally speaking it is important to attack. For the same reason the net player must always be alert, with the racket up, ready to take the shuttle early. If your side has the attack, the player in the rear-court should hit downwards with smashes or drops, trying to create opportunities for the net player to hit winners (see photo 34).

Photo 34 Tian Bingyi and Li Yongbo in the attacking doubles formation. Tian is doing a jump smash; Li is alert in the forecourt

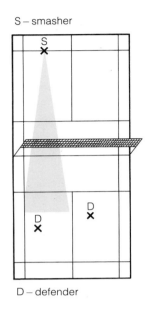

Diagram XX

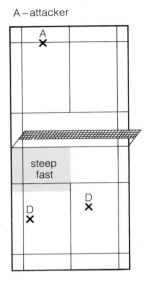

Diagram XXI

The smash

Vary the power, steepness, and placement of the smash. Usually you should smash to the straight player, and best of all at the chest, the inner hip (i.e. on the racket side), or the point where the opponent changes from forehand to backhand. Smashing straight helps your partner, facing forward at the net, to know where the shuttle will be hit to. The net player can then watch the straight defender and move over slightly to that side of the court (see diagram XXII overleaf). If you hit cross-court, you effectively cut your partner out at the net and also open up your own court.

Be wary of smashing down the tramlines even if there appears to be a gap. It is better to aim between your opponents, where both may go for it, or, even better, leave it (see diagram XX).

Drops

Use drop shots as variations but only to the middle or straight – almost never cross-court (see diagram XXI). Steep drops, if deceptive and used in combination with the smash, can be extremely effective. Li Yongbo does it well. Body deception (plus a loud grunt!) can suggest a big smash, and the steep drop comes at the last moment.

The drive

The drive is used much more frequently in doubles than in singles and is played when the shuttle has dropped too low to make contact overhead. It is usually played in the half-court or back-court area and hit from about chest height to pass close to the tape; it can either land deep in the opposing court, or be hit more gently into the opposition's mid-court area.

To produce the shot, whether on the backhand or the forehand, the right foot should step out towards the sideline. On the backhand side it is best to employ a backhand grip. The shoulders turn and the racket is taken back then forward using the forearm rotation and shoulder turn for maximum power. Take the shuttle as high as possible and keep the follow-through quite short. You should be able to recover quickly, pushing off the right foot.

Defensive formation

The basic defence formation is side by side in the mid-court area (see diagram XXII overleaf).

In the diagram the shuttle is about to be smashed from the attackers' forehand court. Defender 'A' is ready to receive a straight smash. Defender 'B' can afford to move towards the centre and slightly closer to the net. 'A' takes smashes down the line and around the body. 'B' covers all smashes to the right of 'A'. This is a general rule and partners need to learn exactly where they

Photo 35 Defensive doubles positions from Eddie Hartono and Sutanto Hadibowo, attacking positions from Tian Bingyi and Li Yongbo. Note the geometry, with all four players moving towards one side and the shuttle having just crossed the net from the backhand corner

expect each others' responsibilities to start and finish, especially with shots between them. Look at photo 35 and notice how all four players have moved towards one side of the court. A variation on defence that can be useful in doubles is the crouch defence (see photo 36).

S and X represents attacking formation
S – smasher
X – smasher's partner

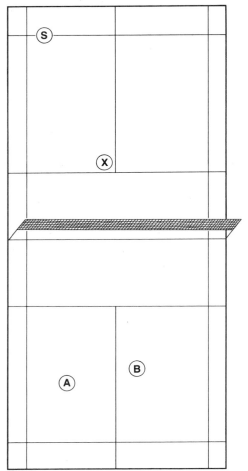

A and B represents defensive formation

Diagram XXII

Photo 36 Liem Swie King playing the crouch defence, partnered by Eddie Hartono

Mixed doubles

In mixed doubles the man is usually stronger than the woman and therefore plays at the back, with the woman at the net. Suitable tactics are developed directly from this. As mixed doubles remains the most popular game at club level it is worth looking at tactics in detail.

Serving position

When the woman serves, the situation is as for level doubles, i.e. server in front of partner. However, when the man serves, the woman still remains in the fore-court in front of her partner. Her role when a low serve is delivered is to cover returns to the fore-court. Therefore, she should remain as central as possible without obstructing her partner's service. This is achieved by placing her feet close to the 'T' and leaning to the appropriate side, which varies according to her partner's service.

When a right-handed man serves forehand, the woman adopts a position in front and to his left for both service courts (see diagram XXIIIa and b). A lefthanded man delivering a forehand service requires his partner in front and leaning to the right.

Coaches used to argue that the backhand serve, while proving superior in level doubles was not suitable for the mixed game. However, in the 1991 World Championships final, both men used backhand serves. While it is not often used in club level mixed at present, it should become more popular in time.

If the woman finds her partner prefers to use a backhand service, she should change the side she leans towards by tilting to her right.

However, some flexibility exists since the backhand is normally delivered from in front of the body. Therefore, the woman may consider leaning to the left side as if her partner was serving forehand. This stance has the advantage of covering

Photo 37 Classic mixed doubles positions: Kim Yun Ja of South Korea, partnered by Park Joo Bong, trying to maintain the attack with a half-court push

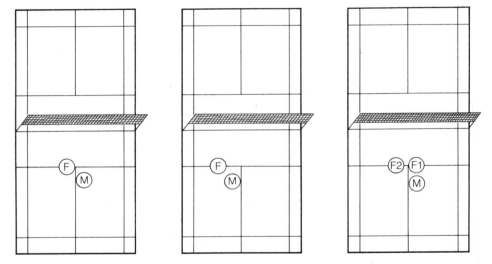

F1 – normal position for partner's
     backhand serve

F2 – possible alternative with
     advantage of covering
     backhand side

Diagram XXIII

her backhand to some extent (see diagram XXIIIc).

While the serving position in mixed doubles can cause problems, the type of service is straightforward. A basic tactic is to pull the opposing man to the net and push the woman to the rear. Therefore, serving low to the man and flicking to the woman is a good strategy.

Receiving (woman)

The woman must expect to receive a lot of flick serves. Therefore, it is sensible for her to adopt a receiving stance some way back from the service line in order to invite a low service. A position up to 1 metre back from the service line is acceptable depending on speed and agility. It is vital that the receiving position chosen enables the woman to

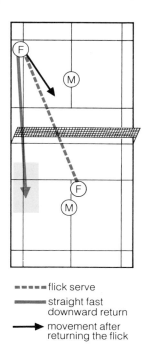

- – – – flick serve
- ———— straight fast downward return
- ——→ movement after returning the flick

Diagram XXIV

get behind a flick serve. This is because she must attempt to hit any flick in a downward direction and then swiftly follow in behind it to take any returns to the fore-court. The best returns of a flick for the woman are to hit a straight smash or fast drop towards the inner tramline (see diagram XXIV).

It is well-worth practising this sequence. Set up a conditioned mixed doubles routine in which the woman practises receiving a flick. She hits straight and downwards and follows in. The opposing man has a choice of returns – straight block, cross-court block (a very good option!) or straight lift. The woman should practise taking any blocks to the net as early as possible and play a kill, net shot or a half-court push. All lifts should be played by her partner. This is very important as this helps the receiving pair to rapidly regain their ideal formation. If the woman answers the straight lift she may find herself pinned to the rear-court with a consequent 'hole' around the net (see diagram XXIV).

Receiving (man)

There is a dilemma for the man in mixed. Should he be aggressive as in men's doubles and try to rush the low serve whenever possible? Or should he play the percentage return to the low serve allowing him time to return to the mid-court while his partner moves towards the net? The best approach is probably a mixture. Adopt an **aggressive** stance so that poor serves can be killed. This has the advantage of intimidating the opposition, in particular the woman, and encourages them to risk a flick serve.

However, if a good service is received, don't be too ambitious. A flat push at the opposing man or a return to the net is risky as it will be easy for the opponents to drive or lift the shuttle to the rear-court, forcing the woman to play the return and stranding the man at the net. A useful return is a half-court push which should allow the receiving

Photo 38 Another South Korean pair, Kim Moon Soo and Hwang Hye Yung, show the classic serving positions for mixed doubles

partnership time to regain the best formation. However, they must be quick. Once the push has been played, the woman should move decisively forward to take any returns to the forecourt and the man must move back to a mid-court base position. An alternative return is a deceptive push (not a lift) to either rear corner which allows the ideal formation to be regained.

General tactics

When the woman is at the net, she should have her racket up and be alert and dominating. She should aim to maintain, or gain, the attack by playing the shuttle downwards with net shots or with delicate pushes into the mid-court area between the opposing players.

When the shuttle is high and the opposition about to attack, the woman should cover the cross-court shot. Therefore a good tactic is for the woman to lift cross-court and the man to lift straight. Diagrams XXV and XXVI show why. Of course, it is better not to lift at all.

If the man has an opportunity to attack, it is often effective to smash at the opposing woman or to drop straight in front of the opposing man – bringing him in to the net. A useful alternative can be a cross-court clear over the woman.

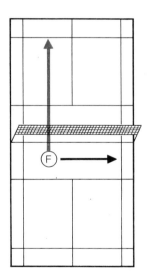

Diagram XXV
If the woman lifts straight she has to change sides to cover the cross-court

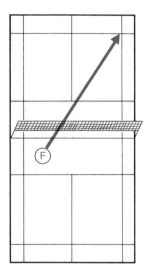

Diagram XXVI
If she lifts cross-court, she is in the correct defensive position

17

TRAINING

Playing badminton is a very enjoyable way of becoming fitter, and many people will not have the time or inclination to undertake additional training.

However, physical fitness is as important a component of a player's ability as shot production.

Warm-up

It is important to warm up gradually before any strenuous activity to prepare the body to function efficiently and reduce the risks of injury.

A full warm-up can take 20–40 minutes. Start with gentle jogging and include movement such as side-steps and backward running for variety. This initial light exercise will raise your body temperature and increase your heart rate which will deliver oxygenated blood to the working muscles.

The second phase of a warm-up involves stretches. These are best performed in a sequence starting from the neck and working down the body and including the arms, waist, legs and ankles. Look at figures 25–30 to see Anne Gibson demonstrating a selection of useful stretches. Pay particular attention to the hamstring and calf muscles.

In a warm-up each stretch should be held for a minimum of 8–10 seconds. For the first few seconds of a stretch, the muscle involved will actually tighten to resist the force. Therefore, holding a stretch for just four or five seconds may be counter-productive, leading to the muscle shortening rather than stretching.

Move into the stretch until you can feel tension in the target muscle and then hold the position while counting out ten seconds (or longer). Do not stretch so far that you are in pain. Stretching should be comfortable. Relax as you hold the stretch and ensure that you breathe normally. Do not be tempted to bounce when stretching; just hold a steady position. As you feel the muscle relax you may be able to stretch further. Repeat each exercise until you feel the muscle is fully stretched.

Once you have completed a thorough stretching programme, start the third phase of the warm-up which involves more vigorous movement. I always do shadow badminton movement at this stage, increasing the speed as I warm up. I include plenty of changes of direction, fast arm movements with the racket and explosive jumps with controlled landings.

Once the three stages have been completed, you will be well prepared to take the court and start hitting shuttles.

Warm-down

This should be performed after any strenuous workout. A warm-down aids recovery by facilitating the removal of waste-products from working muscles.

Gentle jogging and light stretching should be

Figures 25a-d
Stretches for the neck

Figures 26a-b
Stretches for the arms

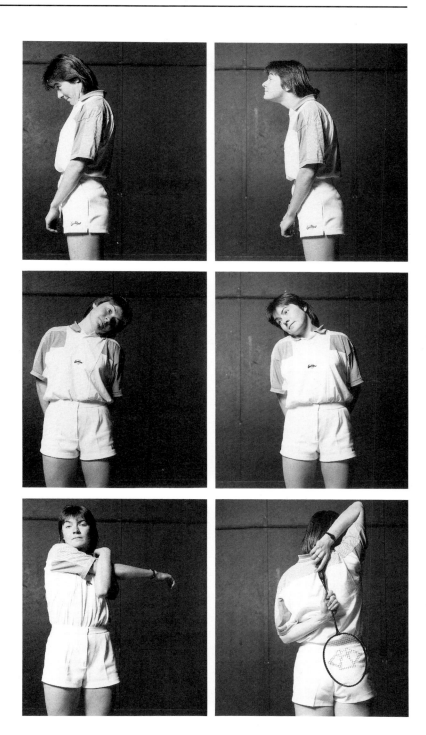

Figure 27
Stretch for the wrist

Figures 28a-c Stretches for the waist

performed for 10–20 minutes so that the body can return gradually to rest.

Flexibility

Flexibility is an important component of fitness, others being speed, endurance and strength. In order to improve flexibility, appropriate stretches need to be held for 20–30 seconds, not for 8–10 as recommended for a warm-up. Competitive players should programme at least three flexibility sessions of 20–30 minutes every week.

Improving flexibility is a gradual process which requires regular work. However, large improvements can be made over a period of just a few weeks.

Endurance

Stamina can be improved by steady runs of 20–60 minutes. You should feel comfortable throughout the run. The aim of this training is to increase aerobic fitness. If you push yourself too hard you are training anaerobically, which is not the intention. At the end of a run you should feel mildly

Figures 29a-f
Stretches for the hamstrings
and upper leg

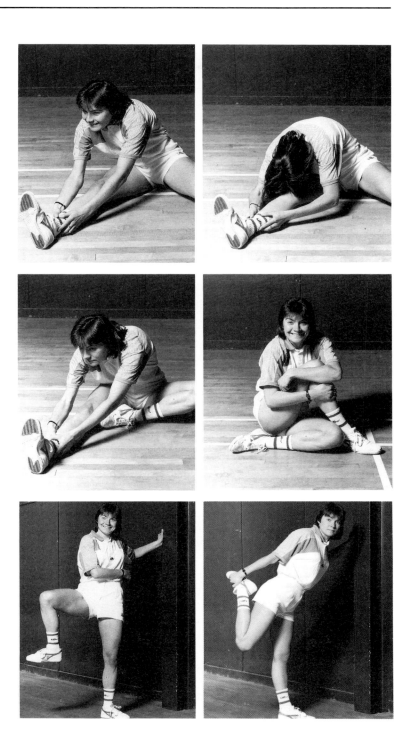

Figures 30a-b
Stretches for calves

mildly tired, not exhausted. If you decide to do some running, then remember:

1. If in any doubt about your fitness, have a medical check-up first.
2. Start with short runs and build up very gradually; walk parts of the run if necessary.
3. Try to breathe deeply but comfortably throughout the exercise.
4. Wear suitable running shoes with plenty of cushioning.
5. If you begin to develop aches or pains, see a physiotherapist.

Another excellent way to improve stamina is to swim. This has the great advantage of putting minimal strain on joints and muscles whilst training the cardio-vascular system.

Strength

The best way to increase strength is by using weights. However, before undertaking any form of weight training the body should be thoroughly prepared through an extensive period of circuit training. Such circuit training should involve all areas of the body, by including exercises such as:

- press-ups
- sit-ups
- dorsals
- burpees
- various jumps

It is not appropriate here to go into detail about weight training. If you are interested in this, obtain advice from a qualified person. However, weight training is not dangerous for adults providing exercises are performed correctly. In fact stronger muscles will help protect joints against injury.

A common belief is that weight training slows people down. In reality an improvement in strength is a prerequisite for improvement in speed.

If you do undertake weight training, the hamstrings and quadriceps are particularly important areas to strengthen for badminton. You will notice in many photographs in this book how well developed players' thigh (or quadricep) muscles are.

A good way to improve leg strength without resorting to weights is to perform jump circuits. These involve a variety of leg strengthening exercises such as:

- lunge jumps
- tuck jumps
- squat jumps
- squat thrusts
- hopping
- bunny jumps

Start off by performing ten of each exercise, resting and stretching between each set. Try to maintain high quality throughout. As your leg strength improves, build up the number of repetitions, and number of sets, and add in extra exercises.

Do not perform any jumping exercises on a hard floor, as this is a sure way to develop shin splints, knee trouble and back pain. A sprung wooden floor, as found on squash courts, is best.

Speed

A useful way to improve speed is fast leg movement exercises. Each of the exercises depicted below can be performed for 5–20 seconds, with various numbers of repetitions. However, speed will only be improved by performing these exercises close to your maximum pace.

Shadow badminton

This involves shadowing or copying badminton movements without a shuttle. Start on the base, move to the front right-hand corner, shadowing a forehand net shot, and then return to the base. This can be repeated ten times at a slow comfortable pace, or five times with more explosion.

Alternatively, build up the sequence to incor-

Figures 31a-e
Forward and back

Figures 32a-b
Together and out

Figures 33a-e
Step-overs

Figures 34a-b
Hip twists

Figures 35a-b
Pivot

Figures 36a-c
Side to side lunge

Figures 37a-e
Stepping over line and back

Figures 38a-b
Lunge jumps

Figure 39

Figure 40

porate a smash followed by a net shot. Or, use all four corners by moving from one to another via the base in a clockwise pattern. The variations are limitless.

The advantage of this form of training is that it is very specific. Not only are you training your body physically, but you are also practising and improving your footwork patterns and stroke actions.

You can train speed or endurance by varying the intensity and number of repetitions performed.

A particularly good kind of shadow badminton involves a coach or fellow player indicating a sequence of movements by pointing to various court positions at random (see figure 39).

Another variation involves collecting and depositing shuttles to and from various parts of the court, using chairs if wished (see figure 40).

Sequence training

Badminton fitness can also be improved by undertaking sequence training. This involves at least two players – one feeding and one working – and in these exercises you will be hitting shuttles, so improving your stroke production as well as your fitness. The feeder hits the shuttle either in a pre-

arranged or random pattern, and the worker returns the shuttle to the feeder's position.

Once again, there are a large number of possibilities. Common, and very useful, sequences are the worker playing a drop shot, followed by a net shot, followed by a drop shot, etc. The feeder stays at the net lifting the first shot and playing a net shot on the next, and so on. You can change the drop shot for a smash (see diagram XXVII).

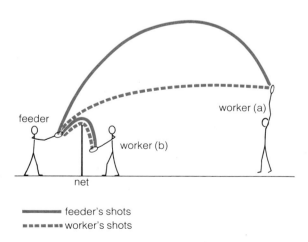

Diagram XXVII

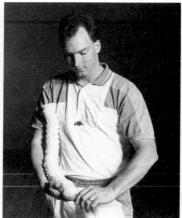

Figure 41a-c

Multi-shuttle work

This is a type of sequence training which involves using a separate shuttle for each stroke the worker makes. One advantage of this is that the feeder can make the worker move at a very fast pace. Multi-shuttle work can involve hand feeding or racket feeding. Figure 41a shows how up to 20 shuttles can be cradled for hand-feeding.

Notice how each shuttle is taken by the cork (figures 41b and c). Look at figures 42a and b to see how multi-shuttle feeding helps Anne Gibson practise her net shots. Downward strokes can be recreated by the feeder standing on a chair (see figures 43a and b).

In order to racket feed it is helpful to have an assistant with the feeder, as shown in figures 44a and b. The assistant, who cradles a quantity of shuttles, must place the base of each firmly into the feeder's non-racket hand. Providing this is done the feeder does not need to look for the next shuttle but can watch the player who is working. (The assistant should not face a worker who is smashing, as this could be dangerous.)

As with sequence work, multi-shuttle routines can be devised to train all aspects of the game.

While it is excellent for training a player at speed, it is also useful for techniques and endurance work if feeding is delivered at a moderate pace.

Daily routine

If time for off-court training is limited I would recommend finding time at least for performing the following exercises:
- sit-ups (see figures 45a and b)
- dorsals (see figures 46a and b)
- leg strength exercises, i.e. a short jump circuit (see section on strength)
- forearm strengthening (see figures 47a and b)

For forearm strengthening, use a racket with a head cover, and shadow various strokes as quickly as possible. Painting a figure of eight in the air in front of you can be a useful exercise.

Figures 42a-b

Figures 43a-b

Figures 44a-b

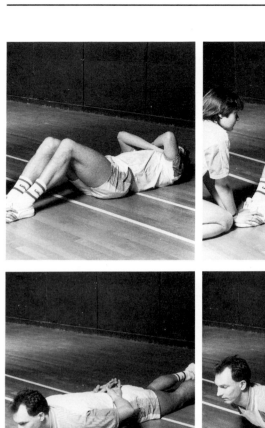

Figures 45a-b

Figures 46a-b

Figures 47a-b

POSTSCRIPT

The advice in these pages should be a guide and not a blueprint. If it can be used that way there is every chance the reader will end up becoming more skilful at badminton. (S)he should also enjoy it more.

In the fullest sense though it will not make a complete player. Badminton is a sport, which implies not only competition but cooperation. There are fundamental areas that cannot be covered by rules of the game or coaching guidelines. If players cannot cooperate and agree on underlying values of fairness and decency, then it ceases to be a sport at all. And eventually the whole magnificent edifice will corrode from within.

To be a complete player therefore means also to have a love of the underlying purposes of the game and a respect for the ethical considerations that helped create it. It means to appreciate the concord that can be made between very different types of people. It means to behave well. It means not knowingly to cheat.

There is no reason why men and women should not play the game hard, without quarter given, and to the limit of the rules. There is no reason why some of them should not earn money from it, occasionally very good money. The professional and the old amateur ideals are by no means completely incompatible.

It is true these ideals have been in conflict in many sports. Badminton, more than most, has retained a wonderful spirit between players whilst making progress towards greater wealth and higher standards. This may or may not continue. It will depend upon the attitudes and character of the players of the future. To them this book is dedicated.